The NICKELODEON™ Guide

TO YOUR BEST-EVER SCHOOL YEAR

BY SUSAN RING

chronicle books · san francisco

Nickelodeon, Nickelodeon All Grown Up, SpongeBob SquarePants, The Adventures of Jimmy Neutron: Boy Genius, The Fairly OddParents, Danny Phantom, Catscratch, Nickelodeon Avatar, and all related titles, logos, and characters are trademarks of Viacom International, Inc. Nickelodeon All Grown Up created by Klasky Csupo, Inc. SpongeBob SquarePants created by Stephen Hillenburg. The Fairly OddParents and Danny Phantom created by Butch Hartman.

Book design by Jessica Dacher.
Typeset in Trade Gothic and Farao.
Manufactured in China.

Library of Congress Cataloging-in-Publication Data
The Nickelodeon Guide to your best-ever school year / by Susan Ring.
p. cm.
ISBN-13: 978-0-8118-5672-0
ISBN-10: 0-8118-5672-0
1. Students—United States. 2. Schools—United States. 3. Academic achievement—United States. I. Title.
LB3605.R455 2007
371.8—dc22
2006014855

Distributed in Canada by Raincoast Books
9050 Shaughnessy Street, Vancouver, British Columbia V6P 6E5

10 9 8 7 6 5 4 3 2 1

Chronicle Books LLC
680 Second Street
San Francisco, California 94107

www.chroniclekids.com
www.nick.com

CONTENTS

What Can This Book Do for ME?

Homework... tests... grades... bullies... embarrassing moments... teacher trouble... friend trouble... after-school overload...

Yup, school life has its fair share of challenges. (Sometimes it feels like an *unfair* share!) But with the book you're now holding, you can figure out how to handle all that.

In these pages, you'll find all sorts of ways to make your day easier—from the time you get up to the time you go to sleep. You'll discover how to zip through the morning so you can get to school on time. You'll get tips on how to face—and *ace*—tests. You'll find out how, when, and where to do your homework and how to make sure you remember all the stuff you need for the next day.

You can read this guide all the way through from beginning to end or just flip to the chapters that interest you most. Any way you use it, this book can help you get through almost any school daze.

Here are just a few places you might want to check out:

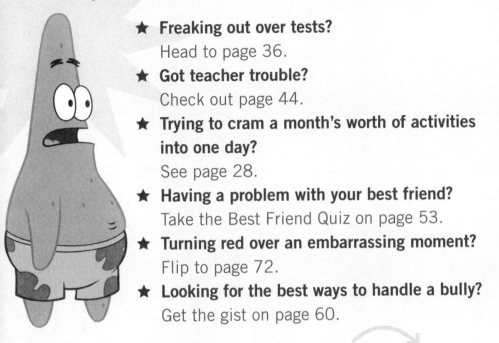

★ **Freaking out over tests?**
  Head to page 36.
★ **Got teacher trouble?**
  Check out page 44.
★ **Trying to cram a month's worth of activities into one day?**
  See page 28.
★ **Having a problem with your best friend?**
  Take the Best Friend Quiz on page 53.
★ **Turning red over an embarrassing moment?**
  Flip to page 72.
★ **Looking for the best ways to handle a bully?**
  Get the gist on page 60.

You'll also find a feature called the Help Hotline. In these sections, you can read about problems kids are having and find out what solutions the Help Hotline suggests. Some of the problems just might sound like ones that you've had yourself!

This guide has lots of other features, too—like quizzes, puzzles, and places to fill in your own experiences and ideas about life at school.

So, crack this book open because school's in session. Hey, you're already on your way to having your...

BEST SCHOOL YEAR **YET!**

CHAPTER 1

Organizing Instead of Agonizing!

SO MUCH TO DO!

Let's face it: School is no small deal. It can be a lot of fun, but it also gives you so much to do and think about—homework, tests, projects, grades, reading assignments...you name it! All of that can keep *anyone* busy!

But then there's life *after* school, too. Maybe you like to play sports or take music lessons. Maybe you're busy helping out at home. And, oh yeah—what about just having *fun* after school? Fitting all of those things into your life can be like trying to cram an elephant into a shoe!

So what's the first thing you can do to make school—and everything you do before and after it—easier? Here are some choices:

- ○ **Memorize the dictionary.**
- ○ **Dance a jig.**
- ○ **Water the plants.**
- ○ **Turn into a goldfish.**
- ○ **Do a cartwheel.**
- ○ **Bake a lasagna.**
- ○ **Get organized.**

If you chose "get organized," you're on the right track. And if you're *already* pretty organized, then you're *definitely* on the right track! But if you're not, don't worry. You CAN get organized, and this chapter will help.

GETTING ORGANIZED: WHAT'S **THAT** SUPPOSED TO MEAN?

Getting organized means figuring out a system that will help you:

★ Know *what* you have to do and *when* you have to do it.
★ Keep track of your stuff, so you have it when you need it.

Organization is the key to getting things done on time, finding things in a jiffy, and just making your life easier!

First, this chapter will show you one great way to stay on top of your assignments, activities, plans, and whatever else you need to remember. Then you'll get some tips on how to deal with all the stuff you need for a day at school. Before you know it, you'll be...

ORGANIZING

INSTEAD OF AGONIZING!

PLAN ON PLANNING WITH A PLANNER

One of the best things you can do to get organized is to get yourself a *planner,* like the one shown below. You can buy planners at school-supply stores, or, even better, you can *create* one with a spiral notebook. Then you can really make it your own! Here's a good way to set up your planner:

	MONDAY DECEMBER 10	TUESDAY DECEMBER 11	WEDNESDAY DECEMBER 12
SOCIAL STUDIES	Review pages 134–150 for test.	Unit test!	Get permission slip signed for museum trip.
MATH		Worksheet (skip #5).	Do page 42, #1–20.
SCIENCE		Come up with project topic.	Go to library after school to get books for project.
READING			Book report due.
	Basketball tryouts all week ⟶ after school.		Bring can for canned food drive.

> Your major class subjects go down the far left-hand column. Each class gets a row where you'll write assignments and reminders.

> For long-term assignments, it helps to plan out the steps you want to take.

> Use the extra space at the bottom for after-school plans, or for reminders for classes you don't have every day.

THURSDAY DECEMBER 13	FRIDAY DECEMBER 14	NOTES FOR THE WEEKEND!
		Make dog costume and fake flowers for play.
Do brainteaser. Study for quiz.	*Quiz on unit 13 today. Do page 45, #11–32.*	
Lab day: Bring baking soda.		
Choose new book. Bring to class tomorrow to share. *Briana's birthday!*		

The five days of the school week go across the top. Three days can go on the left-hand page, and two days can go on the right-hand page.

Use the extra space on the right for weekend plans.

For fun, decorate your planner with drawings, stickers, photos, magazine clippings... whatever you want!

On the following two-page spread in your notebook, you'll create the next week. Make at least four or five weeks at a time, so you can plan ahead!

Your planner can remind you about friends' birthdays, too!

YOU AND YOUR PLANNER

Once you've made your planner exactly the way you want it, you two should become best friends. Take your planner with you to school every day. Look through it often. Make adjustments to it. Treat it well. It'll be there when you need it!

Here's how a day with your planner might go:

★ **At school:** As you get assignments, take out your planner and jot them down. When you find out about a test or a field trip, or any other big event you want to remember, scribble it down.

★ **Before you leave school:** As you load up your backpack, check your planner to make sure you have what you need for your homework.

★ **After school:** Look over your planner before you start your homework, and then check things off as you finish them. You might *add* things to your planner, too, as you look over your assignments. If you have a long-term project, you could break it up into steps and write each step in your planner on the day you think you should have it done.

★ **As you get ready for the next day:** Take one last look through your planner so you know you have all the stuff you need for the next day at school. That way, if tomorrow's a field-trip day and you need to bring a bag lunch, you (hopefully) won't forget!

STUFFING YOUR STUFF

Now that you're an expert on planning with a planner, how about organizing your *stuff?*

WHAT'S IN **YOUR** BACKPACK?

You probably carry a backpack to school every day. It's great to have everything you need in one place. But sometimes it can be a little *too* much of everything in one place!

Here are some ways to make sure you have all of the stuff you need... and none of the stuff you *don't*!

★ **Clean out!** Set aside some time to clean out your backpack at the end of each week. Who knows what treasures you might find? Get rid of old wrappers, crumpled papers, and leaky pens. Check the due dates on any library books you have in there, and return them if you need to.

★ **Store!** Is there stuff you're dragging around that you don't really need anymore, like papers from that science unit you finished two months ago? If so, pull out the old stuff and keep it in a folder at home.

★ **Supply check!** After you clean out, make sure that your supplies are in good working order, and that you have enough of the basics like pencils and paper— but not *too* much! How many sheets of paper do you r*eally* need to carry around every day? The rest can hang out at home for refills, in a supply drawer or box.

PHEW!

DON'T YOU FEEL LIGHTER ALREADY?

HELP! STUFF KEEPS DISAPPEARING ON ME!

Dear Help Hotline,

I keep losing stuff! It's like all my pens and pencils are getting sucked into a black hole. One minute I have a new pencil, and the next minute, it's gone. Just like that! And then I don't have anything to write with for class, and my teacher gets mad, and I have to borrow one. I can tell my friends are getting really sick of loaning them to me. What should I do?

Signed,
Pencil
Problems

Dear Pencil Problems,

Pencils and pens definitely have a way of disappearing! It might help to have a place where you **always** keep your pencils, pens, and other small supplies, like a certain pocket in your backpack that would **only** be for those things. You could even go a step further and put pencils in pencil pouches and put those pouches in your pack! (Say that five times fast!) Either way, it'll definitely help to pick a storage place you'll **always** use, so you'll know where to stash things when you're putting stuff away in a hurry! Then—unless you **really** have pencils with disappearing powers—you'll know where to find your stuff when you need it!

READY FOR **ANYTHING!**

So you've got your new-and-improved, cleaned-out, super-organized backpack... Are you ready to take on the school day?

Here's how to make sure you've got what you need!

★ **Pack up the night before.** If you load up your backpack the night before, you won't have to worry about it in the morning, when you might be in a hurry. So, as you look over the next day in your planner, pack the stuff you need in your backpack. You can also take out the stuff you *don't* need.

Get iceberg model from freezer!

★ **Note to self!** If there's something you *can't* put in your backpack the night before, like a science project that needs to be kept in the freezer, leave yourself a note on the door you'll be leaving through. Then you won't be able to get out the door without remembering!

If you take steps like this before you call it a night, you can rest assured that you're totally prepped for the day ahead. Of course, there are *some* things the school day will throw your way that you could never predict the night before, but if you've got the stuff you *can* expect covered,

YOU'RE DOING A-OKAY!

CHAPTER 2
School-Day Stuff:

How to Be a
Real Class Act

R-R-R-I-N-GGG!!!

RISE AND SHI~~NE~~! SNOOZE

Time to get up! Time to go out and face the day. But sometimes all you want to do is keep snoozin'! What can you do?

This chapter will help you find ways to get ready for the day, to stay focused *during* the day, and to make the best of your time in the classroom. Then you can go from having a sleepy "Patrick" kind of day to one that is a little more "Sandy Cheeks"!

LOSE THE **SNOOZE**

It's tough for many people to get up in the morning for school or work. But it *can* be done. Here are some tricks that might help you bounce out of bed:

★ **Set your clock ahead.** If you set your alarm clock ahead 10 or 15 minutes, when the alarm goes off, it'll actually be a little earlier. That'll help you run on time.

★ **Focus on the fun.** Think about something you're looking forward to that day. That'll help you get out of bed and move full speed ahead.

★ **Say Mmm...** Picture yourself eating something good for breakfast. Maybe you can imagine the smell of a hot waffle with syrup or the yummy taste of a crisp apple. Who would want to stay in bed when *that's* waiting for you?

What's another really important thing that can help you get up and out of bed in the morning? IT'S SIMPLE. You just have to...

MAKE SURE YOU GET ENOUGH SLEEP!

If you don't get enough sleep, you may feel tired, out of it, and not on top of your game. (Unlike SpongeBob, who gets a full eight hours before his fog-horn alarm blows!) Lack of sleep can make it hard to concentrate in class. Simple tasks can seem very difficult. All in all, everything is just plain harder to do.

Why is sleep so important? Look at it as a way to give your body a little vacation. All day long you are going, doing, and thinking. By the end of the day, your body needs a break so it can slow down, rest, and repair itself.

Your brain needs its sleeping time, too. Scientists think the brain uses sleep to sort through information and store memories, and to refuel itself for the next day.

So, even though it seems like you're just shutting down for the night, a lot goes on when you sleep!

BUT HOW MUCH SLEEP IS ENOUGH?

Did you know that cats sleep as much as 18 hours a day? It's amazing that Mr. Blik finds enough time to make trouble!

Do you know how much sleep *people* need? Everyone is different, so there is no set rule. But on average, most adults need seven or eight hours a night. Most young people need even more, like nine or ten hours a night!

BUT WHAT IF I'M NOT TIRED?

It's not always easy to get enough sleep—especially if you get into a pattern of staying up late. Doing these little extras can help you fall asleep more easily:

★ **Relax before you go to bed.** Reading is a good way to unwind.
★ **A warm bath or shower can help, too.** Warm water relaxes your muscles and helps you calm down.
★ **Try to finish eating and exercising several hours before going to sleep.** Running around or having a big meal right before bedtime can get you really revved up!
★ **Keep a routine going.** Go to sleep at the same time each night so your body gets used to the routine and knows when to fall asleep.
★ **And if all else fails...** You can always try counting sheep. Or sponges!

WHAT'S FOR BREAKFAST?

So, once you've had a good night's sleep, what's the *next* thing you need in order to face the day? Breakfast! It's called *breakfast* because it's the first meal you're having after many hours of not eating, or *fasting.* In other words, this is the meal that "breaks" your "fast." And that means it's really important!

Think of it this way: Food is fuel. Just like a car needs gasoline, your body needs fuel to be ready to function throughout the day.

DOES IT HAVE TO BE CEREAL . . . **AGAIN?**

Nope. You can be creative—there's no rule that says you can't microwave a leftover dinner and eat it in the morning! Here are some good breakfast options:

★ **Make the most out of toast!** Spread toast or a waffle with peanut butter. Sprinkle with raisins. Drizzle with honey. Or top your toast with pizza sauce and shredded cheese!
★ **Snack on a sandwich.** Spread cream cheese and jelly on bread for a QBS (quick breakfast sandwich)!
★ **Slurp a yogurt drink.** Or dip into a cup of yogurt.
★ **Pack some protein!** Pour some walnuts, almonds, peanuts, raisins, and granola cereal into a small plastic bag. Shake it up and crunch away!

STAYING FOCUSED

So you made it to school, you're in class, and now it's time to get focused. Is that easy? Not always! Sometimes you have a lot of other things on your mind, and it's hard to stay tuned in on the teacher's lesson. Here are some tips that can help:

★ **Don't just *hear*—listen!** Listening and hearing are not the same thing. Hearing is what your ears do, and listening is what your *mind* does. You really have to make an effort to listen. Focus on the words and really take them in.

★ **Take notes.** As you listen, take notes. Writing things down as you hear them will help you pay attention, stay focused, and also remember things later on.

★ **Ask questions.** If you don't understand something, ask the teacher to explain it. Don't be shy. You might be surprised by how often other kids have the same question in their heads. If there's no time to ask the question, write it in your notes. Then you can ask your teacher after class.

★ **Participate.** During class discussions, chime in! Add comments and respond to things other people say. Being part of the conversation helps you stay focused and interested.

★ **Breathe.** It can be hard for anyone to stay focused for long periods of time. If you find yourself starting to drift off, take a deep breath. Wiggle your toes. Stretch your fingers. These little movements will help get your blood flowing and give your brain a little pick-me-up.

HELP! MY FRIEND IS DISTRACTING ME!

Dear Help Hotline,

My best friend sits next to me in math class. We have a great time together except for one thing: She keeps passing notes to me. I'm dying to read them, but I don't want to get in trouble with the teacher. Plus, I'm not exactly acing math, so I need to pay attention. I don't want to upset my friend, but how do I get her to stop passing me notes without getting her mad? I don't want her to start hanging out with other people just because of some notes.

Signed,
No More
Notes

Dear No More Notes,

You definitely are caught between not upsetting your friend and falling behind in class. But don't worry, there **is** a way to handle this. The best thing to do is to talk to your friend outside of class.

You can let her know that you're very interested in what she has to say, but you just can't talk during class because you're having trouble keeping up, and you're worried about both of you getting in trouble. If she's a real friend, she shouldn't be mad at you for telling her. In fact, she should understand that you **both** would do better in class without the distraction.

IT'S A GROUP THING

Sometimes teachers like to divide the class into small groups to do work during class. That can be a blast if you get a great group that you enjoy working with, but sometimes you end up working with people who aren't exactly focused on getting the job done. That can be frustrating!

Fortunately, there are some things you can do to make working in a group easier and more fun at the same time.

★ **Make sure everyone has a job.** If everyone knows what he or she is supposed to do, then there's less confusion. Here are some possible jobs (you can assign other kinds of jobs based on the specific project):

- The **group leader** checks that all the steps are getting done, leads the discussions, and makes sure everyone is doing his or her assigned task.
- The **recorder** takes notes on discussions or writes down the group's answers and ideas.
- The **reporter** reports to the rest of the class on what your group has done and learned.
- The **timekeeper** keeps an eye on the clock to make sure that you're on track and will finish on time.

★ **Have a big brainstorm!** Once you've settled your group roles, it's time to start work. Depending on your assignment, you may need to start by coming up with lots of ideas, or *brainstorming*. In a brainstorm, people should share ideas without worrying about whether they're good or bad, or whether you'll actually use them or not. One idea can lead to another idea, and that can lead to, well... you never know! (Just ask Jimmy Neutron!) The recorder should write everything down, and then you can decide what to use later. If people are worried about getting criticized for their ideas, you'll have more of a brain*drizzle* than a brain*storm*!

★ **Take turns talking.** Make sure only one person speaks at a time.

★ **Look at the person who is speaking.** Be good listeners.

★ **Make sure everyone participates.** If some people aren't participating, encourage them to do so by asking what they think.

★ **Be respectful if there are problems.** If some people are having trouble staying focused, review what everyone's job is. Offer to help or trade if someone is having a hard time doing a certain job.

★ **Vote!** If you want to make a group decision, take a vote. You can take a secret ballot by writing your votes on scraps of paper, or you can all just raise your hands.

★ **And most of all...**

HAVE A GOOD TIME!

WHEN THE BELL RINGS

Class is over—yes! It's time to grab your stuff and make a mad dash out the door... But wait!

Even though you might *want* to run out the door at full speed sometimes, it's best to take a moment to make sure you're *really* ready to go. Here's a checklist you can run through in your mind to help with that.

Did you...
- ★ write down your assignments in your planner?
- ★ take the books you'll need?
- ★ ask your teacher the questions you jotted down?
- ★ take any printed materials the teacher handed out?
- ★ check in with the people in your group (if you're working on a group project)?

Thirty seconds or a minute is all it might take to do these few things. And that'll help get you out the door in great shape!

CHAPTER 3

Homework Hysteria

CRAMMING AND JAMMING

There are only so many hours in a day. School takes up a large chunk of the weekday, so unless you're able to study, eat, and play in your dreams, that leaves only a few hours to do everything else! How can you cram in all your activities after school and still have time for homework? It's not easy—but this chapter can help you figure it out!

MAKE (AND **KEEP**) A SCHEDULE

It's important to keep track of your time if you're trying to get lots of things done after school. That's why a schedule is so important. Here's how to make one for yourself:

1. **Make a list of what you need to do after school.**
   Homework? Toenail maintenance? Clean your dirt bike? Feed the ducks? Play air guitar?
2. **Decide on the order that you're going to do these things.**
   Think about whether you're choosing the order that you *want* to do these activities or the order you *should* do them if you want to be able to get them all done.
3. **Decide how much time you will give to each activity.**
   You might give yourself an hour to study for a test, a half hour to practice for the spelling bee, and then set aside 20 minutes to work on your radio transmitter to Mars. You'll have paced yourself and finished things that you needed—and wanted—to get done.

MAKE AN EVEN *BETTER* SCHEDULE

If you're really struggling to fit everything in, maybe there are ways to rearrange your schedule that will help you do things more easily. On the next page, you can try your hand at creating your very own new-and-improved schedule.

But just keep in mind, you're not alone—lots of people struggle with not having enough time. Even the author who wrote this didn't have enough time to *fini*

CREATE YOUR OWN NEW-AND-IMPROVED SCHEDULE!

1. Choose your busiest day of the week and write down your normal after-school schedule for that day, from the time school gets out to the time you go to bed.
2. Take a look at the schedule you just made and think about how it could work better for you. Can you pace yourself better? Need to remove something? Maybe you can rearrange your time so you can fit something else in.
3. Now write your new-and-improved schedule.
4. Then try that schedule and see how it works for you. Keep reworking it till you're happy!

OLD
Day: Monday

3:00	Watch TV
3:30	
4:00	
4:30	
5:00	
5:30	Help with dinner
6:00	Dinner
6:30	Practice piano
7:00	Homework and talking
7:30	on the phone with friends
8:00	
8:30	
9:00	
9:30	
10:00	

Here's an example of how a schedule can go from so-so to super!

NEW
Day: Monday

3:00	Homework
3:30	↓
4:00	Ride bike or skate
4:30	↓
5:00	Practice piano
5:30	Help with dinner
6:00	Dinner
6:30	Finish up homework
7:00	
7:30	↓
8:00	Free time to talk on the
8:30	phone, watch TV, read,
9:00	or whatever
9:30	
10:00	

HELP! I'M RUNNING OUT OF TIME!

HELP HOTLINE

Dear Help Hotline,

I have so many things to do during my week that I can't seem to fit them all in. I don't even **like** some of the activities I'm doing right now. I'm taking an art class, working on a magic act, taking drum lessons, playing soccer, and I just joined a bug club. Something's got to give! What should I do?

Signed,
Overwhelmed and
Under Pressure

Dear Over and Under,

Here's a word that might help you: **Prioritize.** It means putting first things first—that is, putting things in order of how important they are. What do you love to do? What do you absolutely **have** to do? Sometimes it's easy to get caught up doing activities because they are more of a habit than a passion. Make a list of your activities. Circle the ones that you can't—or don't want to—give up. Put a question mark next to the others. Talk to your parents about your choices and see if you can work something out to prioritize your schedule.

EVERYONE'S FAVORITE SUBJECT: HOMEWORK!

Now that you've begun to tackle *when* to do your homework, let's take a look at *how* to do your homework. Here are some great ways to make homework more… well… *homey!*

★ **Find a special place to do your homework.** It should be a place where you can concentrate, a place that feels comfortable and where you won't be distracted. Maybe a desk in your room or a favorite spot in the library. Try to use the same space each time. It will put you in homework mode.

★ **Choose great supplies.** If you have notebooks, pens, and pencils that you like to use, the work will be more fun.

★ **Use good lighting.** It's harder and more tiring to work with poor light.

★ **Have some food for thought.** Take a snack with you or eat a light snack right before you sit down to work as an energy boost! Nuts, fruits, yogurt, and good ol' H_2O are excellent brain foods.

MORE HOMEWORK TIPS!

★ **Don't expect to do huge amounts of homework all in one sitting.** Pace yourself. Do a little on the bus. Do a little while waiting for a friend. Little by little, it adds up!

★ **You might even want to set a timer for 30 minutes.** When the timer rings, take a 5 minute break. Walk around; take deep breaths. Then start again.

★ **Set mini-goals for yourself.** For example, decide to finish all your math homework by 4 P.M.

★ **Tackle the hardest stuff first.** That will help make the rest of the assignments a breeze to complete.

★ **If you feel drowsy or start to daydream, stand up and move.** Jog in place. Bend and stretch. Get your blood flowin'.

★ **Reward yourself for a job well done.** Tell yourself that when you've finished all your homework (that's *all* your homework), you will then listen to your favorite song, watch your favorite show, or walk your favorite snail.

★ **Use your handy-dandy planner.** Check and double check that you are doing all the assignments. Then cross each one off as you finish. Wow, that feels good!

THINKING LONG-TERM

When you get a long-term assignment that isn't due for, like, another month, which of the examples below is more like you?

1. You wait until the day before the due date, then get started.
   Result: You're up all night and spend the next day zombie-walking through school.

2. You begin your research right away. You take your time and work on the project over the next month.
   Result: You complete your project without much stress.

So what's the best plan? Start right away, of course! Remember, it's a *long-term* project. That means it's just about impossible to do overnight. Or over two nights. Give yourself time. Use your weekends if you have to (if you start early, you may not have to!). Little by little, it'll get done.

If you can choose your own topic for your project, that's the best situation. Start with something you know and care about. How about your rock collection? That just might turn into a stellar science report. Think about what you have at your fingertips. You might be pleasantly surprised!

{ **CHAPTER 4** }

Let's Examine
Test Time

WHY, WHY, WHY DO WE NEED TESTS?

Why tests? Well, they help you (and your teacher) figure out what you've learned and where your skills lie. They help you move ahead. And, of course, they challenge you.

But they also have a way of stressing you out! That's why it's important to have some strategies that'll help you feel totally prepared, so you can do your best. This chapter will fill you in!

A STUDY IN HOW TO STUDY

Here are three important things to keep in mind as you get ready to study:

1. **Find out exactly what the test will cover.** Make sure you know from your teacher *exactly* what you should focus on. Which set of notes? Which chapters and which concepts?
2. **Make sure you have everything you need to study.** Past tests. Past quizzes. Class notes. Your textbook. Whatever you need, have it on hand.
3. **Plan ahead so you can review over time.** It's better to study over several days than to cram all at once. You'll learn more that way and remember it longer!

MAKING IT FUN

Huh? There are ways to make studying fun? Absolutely. Everybody has a different learning style. Some people learn better by hearing something. Others need to see it. And other people might need to do it or act it out to make it stick.

Here are some fun ways to study. Which one matches your learning style?

★ **Make yourself some flash cards.** Ask your parents to quiz you with them. See how many answers you get right each time you do it.

★ **Be a talk-show guest!** Get together with a friend or sibling. Pretend that your friend or sibling is a talk-show host, and you're the guest. Explain the material you're studying to the host like you're a real expert!

★ **Sing it.** Make up a song about the subject and sing it in the shower... or wherever else!

★ **Write your own story about it.** Studying beetles? Write a story about a beetle and what it eats, looks like, and where it lives, with all the details that will be covered in the test.

★ **Picture it.** If you're reviewing a timeline for history, imagine each event happening in the correct order, like a movie.

MEMORY MAGIC

There's another great way to remember things—it's called a **mnemonic** (neh-MON-ick) **device.** What in the world is a mnemonic device? It's a saying, a rhyme, or another little trick to help you remember something. Here are some examples:

Can't remember the order of the planets? Well, you probably *can* remember this: **M**any **V**ery **E**ager **M**en **J**ust **S**urfed **U**ntil **N**oon. Take the first letter of each word, and you have the first letter of the planets in their correct order.

As a way to remember which months have 30 days, you can say, "Thirty days hath September, April, June, and November."

Mnemonic devices can also be simple little tricks. For example, do you get confused about how to spell *dessert* and *desert?* Just remember that you would want second helpings of a dessert, and that's the word that uses the letter S twice.

MAKE UP YOUR OWN MNEMONIC DEVICES

What do *you* need to remember? Come up with a rhyme or saying or another trick to help you.

NEED TO REMEMBER	MNEMONIC
Which way do you turn a screw to loosen it?	Lefty loosey, righty tighty!

TESTING, TESTING, 1, 2, 3...

Today's the test. You studied, you reviewed, and hopefully you're ready. What else can you do that will make the test taking easier?

★ **Get a good night's sleep before the test.**
Your brain needs sleep to perform well!

★ **Eat a good breakfast.** Remember, food gives you brain power, and you're really going to need your brain today.

★ **Before taking the test, take a couple of slow, deep breaths.** They'll help you relax and bring needed oxygen all through your body.

★ **Think positively!** Picture yourself getting your test back with a big fat A at the top.

★ **Follow directions.** Don't hesitate to ask the teacher if you don't understand something about the directions.

★ **Jot down anything you might forget.** If you're afraid you'll forget some facts or formulas, jot them down on the back of the test or in the margins as soon as you start the test.

★ **Read through the test and make a plan.** Make a mental note of sections that you know will take you longer to do. Answer the easy questions first, then spend time on the harder ones.

★ **When in doubt, don't leave it blank.** Even a partial answer—or a good guess—might get you some points.

★ **Do your best.** In the end, remember that it's a test. It's not your life. And if you do your best, that's all you *can* do!

MAKING THE GRADE

The tests are handed back. You can open your eyes now and look at your grade. Whether you get an A or an F, don't just look at the grade and stop there. Read through your test to find out what you did right and what you did wrong!

Remember, tests can help you learn and move ahead. Learn from your mistakes and your strengths, and you'll probably do even better next time!

AFTER THE TEST

What can you learn AFTER you get a test back? Choose one phrase to fill in each blank.

1. Did you have any trouble following _____ ?
   A. the yellow brick road   B. the directions
   C. the smell of Krabby Patties

2. Do you notice _____ in the mistakes that you made?
   A. patterns   B. a message from Mars   C. bird droppings

3. Were you _____ and too quick to answer some questions?
   A. careless   B. oozing green slime   C. fighting off ghosts

4. Did you _____, or did you run out of time?
   A. burp constantly   B. pace yourself   C. trip on a banana peel

5. Can you see ways that you can _____ next time?
   A. improve   B. build a better toaster
   C. whistle through your nose

CHAPTER 5

Teachers Are People, Too!

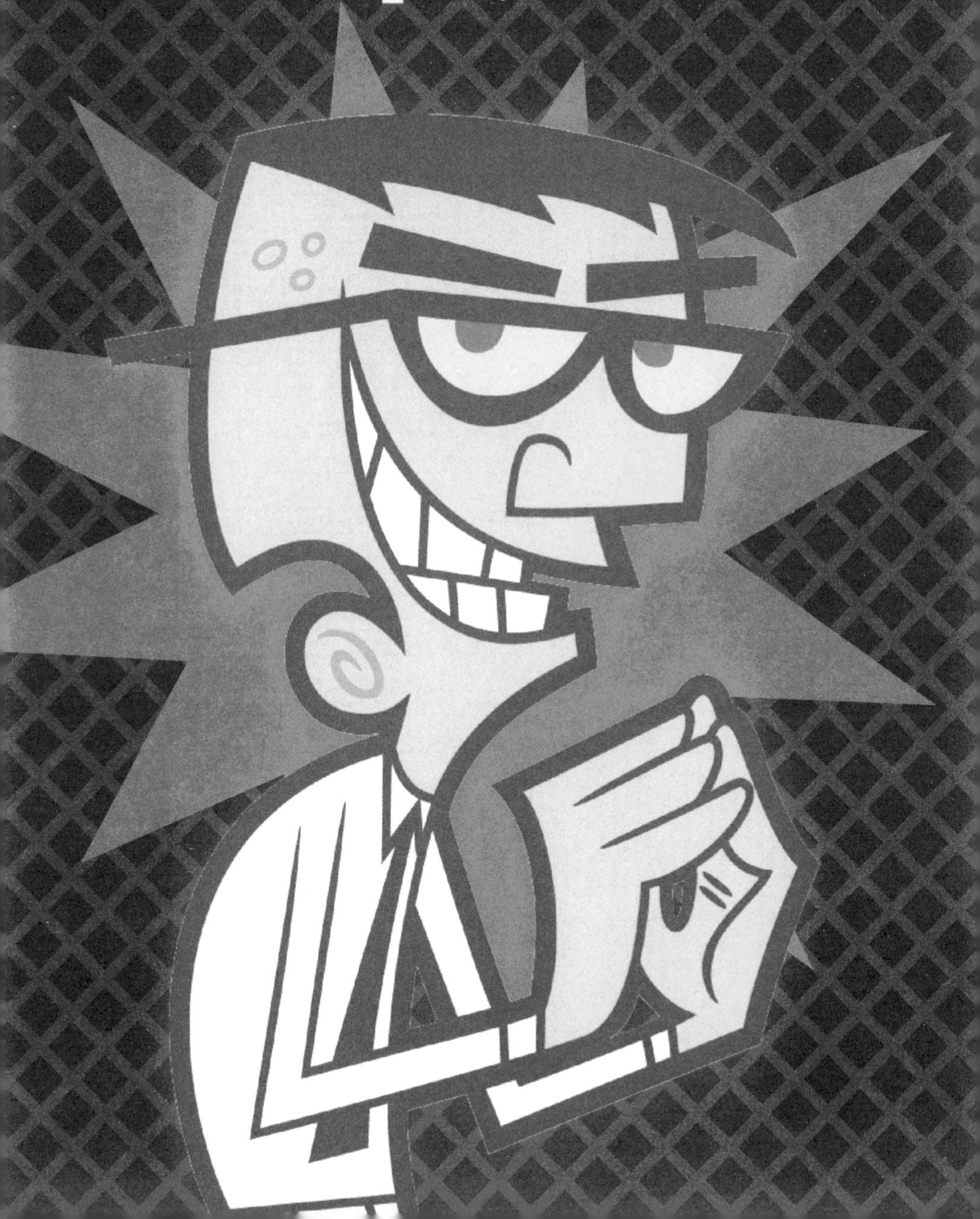

THE **SECRET TRUTH** ABOUT TEACHERS

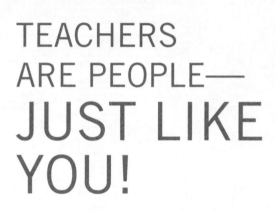

Teachers can be brilliant, so-so, TOUGH, awesome, enthusiastic, and even dull. But no matter their teaching style, here's a little secret that can help you in the classroom every single day:

TEACHERS ARE PEOPLE— JUST LIKE YOU!

REALLY! They have their good days. They have their bad days. They have a life that goes on outside of school. They have things that get them upset and frustrated, and things that make them happy and excited. Remember: Teachers are parents, daughters, sons, brothers, sisters, uncles, aunts, wives, and husbands. And they have feelings and dreams and disappointments just like you do! Keeping this in mind will give you a great advantage.

THE TEACHER AWARDS

Everybody has a gift for doing something outstanding, whether it's tracking down ghosts like Danny Phantom or inventing things like Jimmy Neutron. Even Patrick has a gift of being a true and loyal friend to SpongeBob. Recognizing these things helps us appreciate people for who they are.

Now, think back on the teachers you've had in the past and those you have now. Each one probably stands out to you for having one special gift. So here's your chance to recognize the best. Ready…set…roll out the red carpet and fill in your awards!

FUNNIEST TEACHER

MOST CREATIVE TEACHER

TEACHER WITH THE MOST STYLE

TEACHER WITH THE MOST INTERESTING HOBBY

MOST HELPFUL TEACHER

BETTER RELATIONS

Getting along well with a teacher can make or break a school experience. Here are some things you can do that will help things run smoothly!

Thanks Mr. Lancer for all your help! – Danny

★ **Watch your body language.** Body language can say a lot. Imagine how you would feel at the front of the room looking out into a sea of slouching students. Without words, slouching is telling the teacher you couldn't care less. Sitting up and looking interested will help you connect with the teacher and also help you to focus.

★ **Participate.** Raise your hand when you know the answers. Teachers like students to participate in class and show interest in what they're saying. Also, if you raise your hand when you *do* know the answer, you might not find yourself getting called on unexpectedly when you *don't*!

★ **Ask for extra help.** Whether you're falling behind in your work or just don't understand one minor thing, ask your teacher. Let her know you're interested and want to do better. After all, that's what she wants, too!

★ **Try not to cause disruptions.** Sometimes it might be tempting to goof off, but after a while, constant interruptions can frustrate everybody in the class.

WORDS AND ACTIONS HAVE POWER!

Your choice of words—and actions—can affect your relationships with your teachers. Take this little quiz to see if you get an A in teacher relations!

1. You didn't do your homework. You say:
   A. You always give too much homework anyway.
   B. I had a hard time getting my homework done. What do you think might help?
   C. I'm not the only one who didn't do it!

2. You're asked to stop chatting with a friend in class. You say:
   A. But everyone else is talking!
   B. Sorry about that.
   C. But you didn't *say* we couldn't talk.

3. You're asked to read a book you don't like. You say:
   A. It's boring. I'm not reading it.
   B. I'm having trouble getting into this book. Do you have any suggestions that could help me?
   C. Why can't we pick our own books?

4. You walk into class and your teacher is playing music. You say:
   A. This music is so lame!
   B. I've never heard this music before. What is it?
   C. Where's that horrible sound coming from?

HOW'D YOU DO? So, how many times did you pick choice B? (As you may have guessed—choice B gets you an A in teacher relations!)

HUH?

It happens to everybody. The teacher says something, and you just don't get it. There's nothing wrong with letting the teacher know you don't understand. Most times, lots of other students don't get it either! If you're embarrassed or uncomfortable asking to have something repeated, you can ask the teacher privately after class. The teacher is there to help you. He or she will appreciate the fact that you took the time to really understand something.

Even beyond answering questions, there are *lots* of ways the teacher can help you... if you ask! Teachers will be impressed when you take the initiative (or "act first") to solve problems or improve your work.

★ Another student is distracting you?
   ASK to have your seat moved.
★ Having trouble seeing the board?
   ASK to move closer to the front.
★ Want to bring your grade up?
   ASK to do a special project for extra credit.
★ Need more information on a subject?
   ASK if your teacher knows other sources to go to.
★ Having some issues with a fellow student?
   ASK your teacher the best way to handle it.

BUT I DON'T WANT TO BE A TEACHER'S PET...

Teacher's pet. Kiss-up. Goody-goody. Butter-upper. These are all terms for kids who try really, really hard to get on the teacher's good side. They're usually not too popular with fellow students, though. How, then, can you have a good relationship with your teacher and not end up in the *annoying* category?

You can always be nice and show respect in a *quiet* way. You can go up and talk to your teacher after class. You can hand your teacher a note. You can get to class just a bit early for a short conversation.

The point is not to *show off* how nice you are to the teacher. It's just to *be* nice to the teacher. Remember, teachers are like everyone else—they really appreciate kindness and consideration. How can you make your teacher's day?

★ Ask her about something you know is important to her, such as a vacation or a new grandchild.
★ Know that he likes trains? Show him that old model train you just got.
★ Did your teacher help you get through a difficult situation? Put a thank-you note on his desk.
★ Tell her you're baking for a party. Ask her if she has any recipes to share.
★ Tell him a joke.
★ Ask for advice on how to do better in a tough subject.
★ Discuss a book you love and ask her what some of her favorite books are.

How else can you make your teacher's day? It can be summed up in one word:

RESPECT.

{ **CHAPTER 6** }

Friends Forever

(But Today Doesn't Count)

THE POWER OF FRIENDSHIP

Besides classrooms, teachers, tests, and homework, another big part of school is . . . FRIENDSHIPS!

Friendships are important no matter what age you are. It doesn't matter if you're 8, 32, or 103—everyone needs friends. They give you support, a shoulder to lean on, someone to laugh with, and someone to keep your secrets. They understand, tell you the truth, and want the best for you. So how come sometimes friendships can also be so difficult?

Friendships involve people. Since people aren't perfect, friendships aren't, either. Sometimes people have a bad day. Maybe they're tired. Maybe they're just plain grouchy. On those days, it can be tough to be a friend!

The good news is, there are some things you can do that can help you get through rough times with friends. And that's what this chapter is all about!

WHAT'S ONE LOUSY DAY BETWEEN FRIENDS?

LET IT GO.

WHAT MAKES A GOOD FRIEND?

What do you look for in a friend? Knowing what's important to you can help you develop the friendships that give you those things. On the other hand, you may find that you don't enjoy being with some friends as much as you used to. That could mean that it's time to move on. And that's not a bad thing.

Use the chart below to fill in the positive things that make you happy to be with the friends you have now.

FRIEND'S NAME	WHAT I LIKE ABOUT HIM/HER

Here's what Jimmy might say about *his* friends.

FRIEND'S NAME	WHAT I LIKE ABOUT HIM/HER
Carl	loyal; helps me with experiments
Goddard	best invention I ever made
Cindy	keeps me on my toes
Sheen	good buddy—though obsessed with Ultra Lord!
Libby	calm and mellow

I'M MAD! NOW WHAT?

What's the best thing to do when you're feeling angry at your friend? Sometimes it's hard to know, especially in the heat of the moment! Here's some help:

★ **Hold your tongue when you're boiling over.** If you say hurtful things while you're angry, it might be hard for your friend to forgive you. You can't take your words back, so think hard before you blow up! (Try counting silently to ten before you say something.)

★ **When you're calmer, explain how you feel and why you're upset.** Just be very careful not to attack your friend's personality. In other words, talk about what your friend *did,* not who your friend is as a *person.* For example, you might say, "I was really embarrassed when you laughed at me." Compare that to: "You're a really mean person for laughing at me." The first statement expresses how you felt about what happened and that you didn't like your friend's *actions.* The second is a direct blow to your friend's *personality.*

★ **Be willing to make up.** Don't be afraid to be the first one to say you're sorry. It could go a long way.

★ **Listen to your friend.** Don't shut him out when he tells you why he's angry, too.

THE BEST FRIEND QUIZ

Take this quiz to find out if your best friend has what it takes!

1. My best friend can keep a secret. TRUE / FALSE
2. When I'm feeling down, my best friend comforts me and doesn't criticize me. TRUE / FALSE
3. My best friend understands my sense of humor. TRUE / FALSE
4. My best friend and I share ideas and make decisions together instead of one person just bossing the other around. TRUE / FALSE
5. My best friend is honest with me. TRUE / FALSE
6. My best friend listens to me and remembers things I say. TRUE / FALSE
7. My best friend makes me feel welcome to join in when he or she is with other friends. TRUE / FALSE
8. My best friend supports and encourages me instead of competing with me. TRUE / FALSE
9. I feel good after spending time with my best friend. TRUE / FALSE
10. I trust my best friend. TRUE / FALSE

If you answered "TRUE" to 9–10 of the questions:
You are a lucky friend! Your best friend has what it takes!

If you answered "TRUE" to 6–8 of the questions:
You have a pretty good friendship, but it needs a little work.

If you answered "TRUE" to JUST 1–5 of the questions:
Hmmm... It might be time to rethink this friendship.

DID YOU HEAR?

Did you hear that…gossip can really mess up a friendship? It's often tempting to be part of the gossip, because it can make you feel bonded with the people you're talking with at the time. But in the long run, it doesn't do you—or anybody else—any good. When it comes to gossip, here are some important things to keep in mind:

★ **Trust is probably the most important part of any friendship.** Your friends need to know that the private things they share with you *today* won't become *tomorrow's* juicy gossip!

★ **Gossip hurts people, and it can come back to hurt you, too.** No one wants to be the topic of someone's gossip. And if people are chatting away about someone else, they could very easily put you in the gossip hot seat at some point.

★ **Be careful what you e-mail!** E-mail spreads the word like wildfire. People can easily forward your e-mail, and you can never take those words back.

★ **If your friends are gossiping, try to change the subject, or come up with an excuse to leave.** Being away from it takes away the temptation to join in!

HELP! I LOST MY FRIEND!

Dear Help Hotline,

Now that I'm in middle school, my best friend has dropped me. He sits with all new kids at lunch, and he hardly ever talks to me anymore. Guess I'm not cool enough or something. I've made some other new friends, but I still feel upset. I just can't believe he could go from being my best friend to totally ignoring me!

Signed,
Dropped

Dear Dropped,

It can certainly be painful to lose a close friend like that. If you've tried to talk to him about it and he still ignores you, it's probably best to just leave it be. You don't need a friend like that. What you **can** do is move on and get to know these new kids you like. The more you start hanging out with other friends, the less this will hurt. You might just make a better best friend!

LONELY NO MORE!

Are there days when you find yourself sitting alone at lunch? Times when you end up alone at break time or recess? It can happen. Instead of being embarrassed, try this: Do your own thing! Who cares what people think.

You can:
- ★ Listen to music.
- ★ Make sketches in your notebook.
- ★ Write a story.
- ★ Read a book or a magazine.
- ★ Do a crossword puzzle.
- ★ Practice a magic trick.
- ★ Fold an origami dragon...or whatever!

Get involved in something *you* like to do. That might even draw people to you. They'll be wondering what you're doing, and they'll be thinking how cool it is that you're so confident, creative, and interesting!

{ CHAPTER 7 }

Bullies: You Talkin' to Me?

TOUGH STUFF!

OUCH! Bullies can be tough to deal with. They can make going to school a total nightmare! This chapter will give you some tips on how to handle bullies—but first and foremost, if a bully is bothering you, your best move is to get **adult help.** Whether it's a parent, a teacher, a counselor, or a principal, look for someone you can turn to when the going gets rough, so you don't have to go it alone.

WHAT DO BULLIES LOOK LIKE?

There's no typical look for a bully. A bully doesn't have to be a huge guy with giant arms and a humongous head. A bully can be a small girl with cute little curls.

A bully can be a tiny invertebrate...

... or a cat with pointy ears!

It's how someone *acts* and what that person *says* that makes him or her a bully.

What's the difference between being a leader and being a bully? Listening. Compromising. Being kind. That's what leaders do.

Can you recognize when someone's being a bully? See if you can circle all the "bully talk" on the next page.

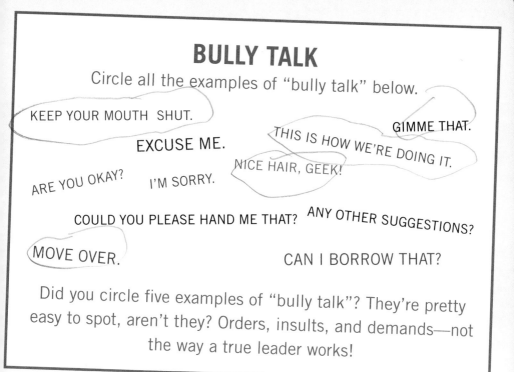

BULLY TALK

Circle all the examples of "bully talk" below.

KEEP YOUR MOUTH SHUT.

GIMME THAT.

EXCUSE ME.

THIS IS HOW WE'RE DOING IT.

NICE HAIR, GEEK!

ARE YOU OKAY?   I'M SORRY.

COULD YOU PLEASE HAND ME THAT?   ANY OTHER SUGGESTIONS?

MOVE OVER.   CAN I BORROW THAT?

Did you circle five examples of "bully talk"? They're pretty easy to spot, aren't they? Orders, insults, and demands—not the way a true leader works!

WHY BULLIES BULLY

If you could crawl inside the mind of a bully, what would you find out? You'd probably discover that bullies are really very insecure. Most people who turn out to be bullies have suffered themselves from someone mistreating them. They don't know any other way to protect themselves. They only feel secure if they have power.

It's sort of as if they're saying, "I'll bully you before you find out how weak and insecure I really am." Somehow, getting you to react, or be fearful, makes them feel better.

Sometimes it may seem like a bully is "popular" with other kids, but often that's just because the kids are afraid of her! A person can be popular because she's nice, thoughtful, and kind.

YOU'RE NOT THE BOSS OF ME!

Don't ever blame yourself for being bullied. A bully doesn't need a reason to be mean. In fact, this just about sums it up:

QUESTION: WHY DO BULLIES BULLY?
ANSWER: BECAUSE THEY CAN.

So let's look at how to make it so they *can't* and *don't!*

★ **Consider the source.** Do you really care what this person thinks of you, or thinks in general?
★ **Set boundaries.** Be sure about what you will and will not put up with.
★ **Ignore, ignore, ignore.** Bullies want to get a rise out of you. After a while, when they see that they can't, they'll probably get bored and leave you alone. The only thing here is being able to wait it out and be consistent. Keep track of the days that you're bothered by a bully. See if the problem starts to decrease once you stop reacting.
★ **Act calm.** Again, the bully wants to get a rise out of you. Don't give it to her. It's best not to act scared (even if you *are* trembling in your boots). If you do speak to the bully, speak in a soft, firm voice. Don't whine or cry or throw a fit. That will only make things worse!
★ **Avoid the bully.** Figure out ways to avoid crossing paths with the bully—especially when you're alone!
★ **Get help from an adult.** Don't ever be ashamed to get an adult's help, whether it's a principal, a teacher, a bus driver, or a parent. And if there's a reason why you're afraid to get help (because you don't want the bully to know you told on him), make sure to explain that. Work with the adult to find a way to help that won't make things worse!

Dear Help Hotline,

A kid in band class picks on me, calls me names, and sometimes even hides my guitar. I try to ignore him, but when he hides my guitar, I have to react. And yes, I already told the teacher, but it didn't do any good. Got any advice on how to make him leave me alone?

Signed,
Picked On

Dear Picked On,

You're doing the right thing by trying to ignore this bully—but it sounds like that's not enough. It sounds like you need to talk to your teacher **again.** The teacher might not realize that the problem hasn't been resolved. Explain that you need to move your seat, or do whatever else you can do to make sure you and your guitar will be nowhere near this bully. And ask the teacher to make sure there are stiff consequences if the guitar ever gets taken again.

Then, keep your focus on the guitar and practice, practice, practice. Become a great guitar player—that will be the best revenge of all!

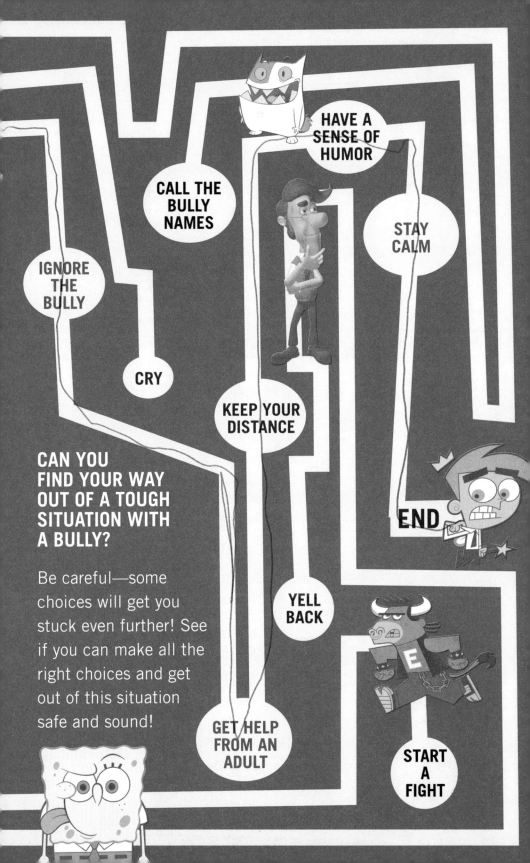

HAVE A SENSE OF HUMOR

CALL THE BULLY NAMES

STAY CALM

IGNORE THE BULLY

CRY

KEEP YOUR DISTANCE

CAN YOU FIND YOUR WAY OUT OF A TOUGH SITUATION WITH A BULLY?

Be careful—some choices will get you stuck even further! See if you can make all the right choices and get out of this situation safe and sound!

END

YELL BACK

GET HELP FROM AN ADULT

START A FIGHT

YOU HAVE THE POWER

So, did you find your way out of the bully maze?

The biggest thing to remember is that you always have a choice in how you respond to a bully. No one can *make* you act a certain way. You have the power to find your way out—and to get *help* finding your way out if you need it!

THE WRITE THING TO DO

When you're going through a tough time, whether you're dealing with a bully or some other problem, keeping a journal can help. Getting your thoughts and feelings on paper really *can* make you feel better!

Writing in a journal allows you to look at your situation more clearly. Sorting out your thoughts and feelings can also help you feel more in control. Then, when you ask for help from an adult, you can explain your situation from a place of strength.

Reading your own journal also helps you to look back on a situation, figure out what worked for you and what didn't, and see if things have changed.

Your journal doesn't have to be fancy. It can be a simple notebook. Just enter the date on top of the page, and then begin! Remember... It's all to help you feel better, and it's for your eyes only!

CHAPTER 8

Peer Pressure: How to Deal

UNDER PRESSURE

What makes you happy?
REALLY HAPPY?

Do you like to do science projects?
Hunt for ghosts? Go jellyfishing?

There are probably *lots* of things
you like to do. But are there times
when you do things because you think
your friends want you to? Maybe you feel
pressured to act a certain way because your friends are acting
that way, but really it makes you feel kind of uncomfortable?

That's called *peer pressure,* and it can sometimes steer you
away from the things that make the real you really happy!

STAYING TRUE TO THE REAL YOU

It can be tough to stay true to the real you when you feel a lot
of pressure to act like everyone else! How much do you feel the
pressure? Try the quiz on the next page and see!

HOW DO YOU HANDLE THE PRESSURE?

Read each of the statements below and give yourself a 1, 2, or 3:

1 = often   **2 = sometimes**   **3 = never**

☐ 1. I hang out with people I don't like that much just because they're popular.

☐ 2. I ignore some of my less popular friends whenever the really cool, popular kids are around.

☐ 3. I join in activities that I don't really enjoy because they're "cool" things to do.

☐ 4. I act up in class to give my friends a good laugh.

☐ 5. I drop activities I like because I worry that they're not so cool.

☐ 6. I join others when they do something I feel is wrong because I want to be part of their group.

☐ 7. I won't wear clothes that I like because I'm afraid people will think they're weird.

☐ **TOTAL HERE!**

Now add up your score, then turn the page to see how you did!

HOW'D YOU DO?

7–14: Time to look more closely at what you like and what you think is right, and work harder at being true to yourself!

15–18: You're on your way to being true to yourself. Remind yourself to keep your focus on what *you* want, not what the crowd expects!

19–21: Good for you! You're aware of the real you and don't let peer pressure take control.

YOUR BEST BUD

Who's the very best friend you have? You! Your relationship with yourself is one of the most important relationships you'll ever have. Here are some other things to think about to help you be your own best friend:

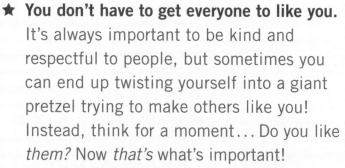

★ **You don't have to get everyone to like you.** It's always important to be kind and respectful to people, but sometimes you can end up twisting yourself into a giant pretzel trying to make others like you! Instead, think for a moment... Do you like *them?* Now *that's* what's important!

★ **Everyone has insecurities.** You might wish you were tall like Jenny, but at the same time, she just might be wishing she was small like you!

★ **An individual style *is* cool!** It proudly shows people who you are. Maybe you're artistic, carefree, neat, funny... Let it show!

HELP! MY FRIEND IS ALWAYS TRYING TO FIX ME!

HELP HOTLINE

Dear Help Hotline,

I have this friend who I really like, but she keeps bugging me to get a new haircut. I like my hair long like it is. She also told me the other day to wear more skirts, that I shouldn't wear so much green, and that I should get a new coat. What should I do?

Signed,
Bugged and Confused

Dear Bugged and Confused,

Know what you **really** need to get? A new friend!

GET CONFIDENT

It's not easy to resist the power of peer pressure—it takes a strong, confident person to do that! Here's what it means to be confident:

I AM CONFIDENT! I AM ...

C = **C**apable
O = **O**pen to new things
N = **N**ot afraid to be different
F = **F**ull of my own ideas
I = **I**maginative
D = **D**aring
E = **E**nthusiastic
N = **N**ot perfect
T = **T**otally fine being me

Now try doing this with the letters in your name. Just write your name vertically down the side of a sheet of paper, and then, for each letter, come up with a word or phrase that describes YOU. How many wonderful things can you come up with?

In the end, remember: It's *who you are* that counts. Not what you wear, where you live, what instrument you play, or what gadgets you have.

YOU'RE GREAT JUST BEING **YOU!**

CHAPTER 9

Embarrassing Moments:

Flushing and Blushing

UGH!!

Picture this. Some guy in your class goes up to write on the board and accidentally farts! You immediately start laughing. The whole class gets a big kick out of it. Everybody, that is, but the guy who *foofed.* Now picture this:

THAT PERSON AT THE
BOARD IS **YOU!**
UGH!
HOW EMBARRASSING!

Embarrassing moments like this can be totally awful. They can make anyone want to crawl in a hole or become invisible. When you spend so many hours of the day in school, moments like these are bound to happen. But remember, everybody makes mistakes and gets into embarrassing situations. Presidents trip, athletes spin out, and even television stars mess up their lines.

WHAT TO DO?

How do you recover in these types of situations? You can't make it go away or pretend it never happened. You can't ask your fairy godparents to rewind time or erase everyone's memory! But what you *can* do is get through these situations with dignity and grace. Check out the quiz on the next page, and see if you can figure out how to respond to each situation!

SOOOO EMBARRASSED!

Look at this list of some moments that can be quite uncomfortable (to say the least!). Which response do you think is best?

1. As you go up to sharpen your pencil, you let one rip in front of the class. You:
   A. Say, "Excuse me" and keep walking.
   B. Say, "Whoops" and laugh with everyone else.
   C. Smile and say, "Anyone want an encore?"

2. You realize that the boy you have a crush on heard you telling your friend how cute he looks today. You:
   A. Turn to him and say, "Yup, still lookin' sharp."
   B. Smile and say, "Consider yourself complimented."
   C. Grin and ask, "Wasn't that nice of me to say?"

3. As you're walking toward that cute girl you like, you trip on your own shoes and fall by her locker. You:
   A. Get out a tissue and pretend you're cleaning the floor.
   B. Stand up and say, "If Niagara Falls, then why can't I?"
   C. Just laugh!

4. You make more noise than a marching band in the bathroom stall and when you come out you realize you have an audience. You:
   A. Just go about your business and remember that even beauty queens use the bathroom.
   B. Laugh and say, "Wow, that was some spicy chili!"
   C. Point back to the stall and say, "I wouldn't go in there if I were you!"

HOW'D YOU DO?

If you answered A, B, or C to any of the situations in the quiz, you would have been correct. You see, there's no rule book that teaches you how to behave when you're embarrassed. It's an "in the moment" kind of thing. You can't plan for it. All you can do is keep your dignity, have a sense of humor, and remember that everyone (EVERYONE!) gets embarrassed by one thing or another!

PIMPLES AND OTHER BUMPS IN THE ROAD

As you grow and mature, your body starts changing, too. One of the things that just about every single person faces at some point in his or her life is... zits!

Zit. Pimple. Blemish. Any way you say it—those things that pop up on your face can make you want to hide. But the most important thing to realize here is that people are often their own harshest critics. You may have a pimple that drives you crazy, but no one else might even notice it!

So, how can you deal when you have a pimple? Ask your parents if they have some tricks to suggest— they've had to deal with pimples, too! But the main thing to remember is that it's probably not as bad as *you* think it is! Movie stars and models appear to never have any zits. Well, guess what? They have makeup artists to help them, and their photos are often touched up to look perfect. No one... (repeat)... *no one* is perfect.

PUBLIC SPEAKING AND FREAKING

Did you know that public speaking is most people's number-one fear? You may someday have to speak in front of a group. Perhaps you won an award or ran for student government and have to give a speech. How in the world are you going to get through it without freaking out?

The good news is that the more you do it, the less scary it'll be. Remember the two *P*'s: PREPARE AND PRACTICE.

Say your speech in front of the mirror. Say it to your family. Tell it to your dog. Practice it in the shower. The more you prepare, the less scary it will be.

You may start out nervous (even famous actors still get nervous before going on stage), but once you begin speaking, try to get involved in what you're saying. Concentrate on the words themselves and the meaning behind your speech.

THAT SHOULD CARRY YOU THROUGH RIGHT TO THE
END!

HELP! I CALLED HER MOM!

Dear Help Hotline,

I can't believe what I did today. I raised my hand in English class and instead of saying, "Mrs. Oaks," I said, "Mom." Well, the whole class cracked up. I wanted to crawl under my desk and disappear. What could I have done?

Signed,
Not Her Son

Dear Sonny Boy,

You can often get out of an embarrassing situation by laughing along with everyone else. Sometimes it's easier just to admit that you did something goofy. You might laugh and say something like, "Why did I say that? That was weird."

Or you might take what you said and really exaggerate it. For example, you might say something like, "Now that I called you Mom, what's for dinner?" It's hard to be the subject of a joke, but in this case it doesn't sound like they were laughing at you, only at a silly situation.

CHAPTER 10

Making Your School Better:

It Starts with You!

WHAT CAN **YOU** DO?

There are so many ways you can make this your best school year ever. One way is to help make the *school itself* a better place to be and to learn. You can complain and complain that things just aren't right in your school. But does that help anything? NOT REALLY. Here's a better idea. To make your school better, be part of the SOLUTION!

RUN FOR OFFICE!

Take the driver's seat when it comes to making change and run for student government.

The student government can do all sorts of creative things to make school more fun. They can hold dances, parties, and contests. They can raise money to bring a guest speaker to your school or to pay for a field trip.

You don't have to do the ordinary bake sale or car wash to raise money. Be creative! Be wacky! Here are some great fund-raising ideas. Charge even a small admission to any of these events, and you'll be bringing in the dough before you know it!

★ **Hold a karaoke singing contest.** Choose a panel of three judges to give their comments.
★ **Have a talent show.** Roll out the red carpet and sell tickets and refreshments.

★ **Try a "Guess the Baby" contest.** Get your teachers to bring in their baby pictures and post them on one large board. Anyone who wants to guess who's who has to buy a ticket!

★ **Dance for hours.** Hold a dance-a-thon. Everyone who dances has a sponsor, and the sponsor pays a certain amount of money for every minute (or hour) danced.

LET'S GET BUSY!

Beyond making money for *fun* things, your student government can take action on issues that you care about. Want to hold a canned food drive for the local shelter? Clean up a local park or beach? Collect toys or clothes for needy kids? Read to people in hospitals or nursing homes? Write letters to kids in other countries? It's up to you!

START A CLUB

You can also get involved by starting a club. Do you love to read? Begin a book club. Want to protect the wetlands behind the school? Start a nature club. Learning how to draw cartoons? Start a comics club. Begin a Bikini Bottom fan club! The options are endless, and you don't have to wait for someone else to do it. Decide what you'd like to do. Ask one of your favorite teachers to supervise your meetings. Make sure you have the okay from the powers-that-be at your school, and then spread the word!

Bikini Bottom
Fan Club Meeting
TODAY!
room 213 at 3:30

congratulations!

YOU MADE IT! You now have tons of tips and tools to improve your time in school! Whether you want to form better study habits or form a club, this book is here to help you and *keep* helping you. Use it over and over again to refresh your memory and guide you through your school days!

As you go through the school year, there will always be surprises along the way, but having the skills you learned in this book can only help make this your...

BEST-EVER SCHOOL YEAR!

This certifies that

YOUR NAME HERE

completed this book on

DATE

and is on the way to having a **super-amazing-great-fantastic-o** school year.